Color The Story of Christmas

This Book Belongs to:

Published 2015 by Concordia Publishing House
3558 S. Jefferson Avenue, St. Louis, MO 63118-3968
1-800-325-3040 · www.cph.org

Concordia
Publishing House

Jesus Is Our Savior

The Road to Bethlehem!

Close your eyes and have someone talk you through the maze! You'll have to trust them to guide you all the way there! Then open your eyes and see how good you and your partner work as a team!

Start

Finish

This Is the Story of
Jesus

Code Words!

Each number represents a letter of the alphabet. Insert the correct letter over each number to find a hidden message from the Bible to you!

A	B	C	D	E	F	G	H	I	J
1	2	3	4	5	6	7	8	9	10

K	L	M	N	O	P	Q	R	S	T
11	12	13	14	15	16	17	18	19	20

U	V	W	X	Y	Z
21	22	23	24	25	26

—— —— —— —— ——   —— —— —— —— ——   —— —— ,
10 5 19 21 19   12 15 22 5 19   13 5

—— —— —— ——   ——   —— —— —— ——
20 8 9 19   9   11 14 15 23

Zechariah Was a Priest

Follow the Letter Trail!

Follow the trail of letters that spell J-E-S-U-S-L-O-V-E-S-M-E
to get out of the maze! You can go up, down, left or right.

START HERE

```
J  E  S  F  H  S  C  H  Q  U  R  D  G  U  A  D  C  B  G  J
P  Y  U  W  V  E  S  L  A  J  E  L  O  K  D  E  S  K  T  K
L  V  S  L  O  I  M  O  Z  E  S  V  S  H  M  E  J  E  L  U
M  D  L  T  G  K  E  U  X  M  U  O  V  E  S  C  H  S  G  G
K  S  O  V  A  D  J  I  E  S  S  L  O  E  M  E  S  U  D  B
O  R  N  E  M  E  E  E  V  S  G  O  A  E  V  O  L  H  E  G
I  Y  N  D  B  G  S  F  O  W  S  D  S  S  O  J  E  F  S  V
J  J  E  Z  S  S  U  S  L  O  W  D  E  M  V  M  E  D  C  V
N  E  I  S  X  U  J  E  C  C  L  I  H  E  J  O  S  O  K  F
B  S  A  D  E  O  A  S  E  A  M  E  D  G  E  S  U  S  L  R
H  L  D  R  V  I  L  L  S  H  G  N  S  E  J  E  S  L  O  T
U  O  M  G  L  K  I  U  S  E  I  R  U  D  L  M  S  E  V  G
Y  M  E  J  R  F  C  N  M  V  O  L  S  M  J  H  G  H  O  B
E  G  J  U  D  H  D  W  E  P  B  A  L  M  S  L  E  S  U  N
T  T  O  K  J  N  G  G  J  E  E  O  E  S  M  E  J  V  S  H
F  J  J  X  C  V  B  N  M  S  U  S  V  U  U  M  E  E  L  Y
G  A  S  D  F  Q  U  K  D  L  S  L  O  L  O  S  E  V  O  U
V  U  L  D  G  H  J  I  V  D  H  T  V  J  E  M  M  S  J  J
C  A  R  F  I  K  L  P  S  W  H  T  B  N  M  E  M  U  P  M
```

FINISH HERE

Zechariah Sees an Angel

Word Search

B	K	I	B	Y	G	R	D
O	H	S	E	D	I	L	J
R	K	G	I	F	T	S	E
N	N	V	E	D	T	T	S
A	N	G	E	L	A	A	U
W	E	R	G	Y	J	R	S
A	N	G	I	K	L	O	P
L	M	A	N	G	E	R	S

WORDS TO FIND:

JESUS	BORN	STAR
MANGER	GIFT	ANGEL

Zechariah Cannot Speak

Using only the letters in the words below, how many other words can you make?

Zechariah, Elizabeth, and John

_____   _____

_____   _____

_____   _____

_____   _____

_____   _____

_____   _____

_____   _____

_____   _____

_____   _____

_____   _____

The Angel Gabriel Appeared to
Mary

Bible Trivia Page!

See how many Bible Trivia questions you can answer!

1. Jesus' mother was named _____.

2. Jesus was born in the town of _____.

3. Jesus called a total of _____ (number) disciples.

4. Name three of Jesus's disciples.

5. Jesus fed _____ people with a little boy's lunch.

She Will Be the Mother of
Jesus

Code Words!

Each number represents a letter of the alphabet. Insert the correct letter over each number to find a hidden message from the Bible to you!

A	B	C	D	E	F	G	H	I	J
11	19	4	9	14	3	6	18	13	2

K	L	M	N	O	P	Q	R	S	T
23	17	5	22	10	24	12	1	16	21

U	V	W	X	Y	Z
15	25	7	20	8	26

_3 10 1_   _6 10 9_   _16 10_   _17 10 25 14 9_

_21 18 14_   _7 10 1 17 9,_   _18 14_   _6 11 25 14_

_18 13 16_   _10 22 17 8_   _16 10 22,_   _16 10_

_21 18 11 21_   _7 18 10 14 25 14 1_   _19 14 17 13 14 25 14 16_

_13 22_   _18 13 5_   _7 13 17 17_   _18 11 25 14_

_14 25 14 1 17 11 16 21 13 22 6_   _17 13 3 14._   -John 3:16

Elizabeth
Was Zechariah's Wife

COUNT HOW MANY FIGS FELL OUT OF ELIZABETH'S BASKET!

Will you help Mary?

Help Mary find the way to Elizabeth's house.

Mary Thanked God For Blessing Her

Tic-Tac-Toe

One player is X, the other player is O. Take turns marking in one of the
nine squares on the board. First to get three in a row wins!

winner _____

winner _____

winner _____

winner _____

Zechariah Trusted God With All His Heart

The Great Word Scramble

Using only the letters in the words below,
how many other words can you make?

JOHN THE BAPTIST

Elizabeth Named Her Baby
John

Follow the letters to find the name of the baby in the crib.

Start here:

H A Q W E R T Y U

A I S D F G H J K

L Z S N A M E X C

V B N M Q W I E R

T Y U I O P S A S

D F G H J K J L Z

X C V B N O B N M

Q W E R H R T Y U

I O P N A S D F H

John Was a Special
Blessing

The Great Dot Game!

Each player must draw a line (up and down or side to side, no diagonals) to connect 2 dots on the board. If a player's line closes a square, then they recieve 1 point. If you close a box, you get to draw another line! Write your initials inside any closed boxes to keep track of how many points you have!

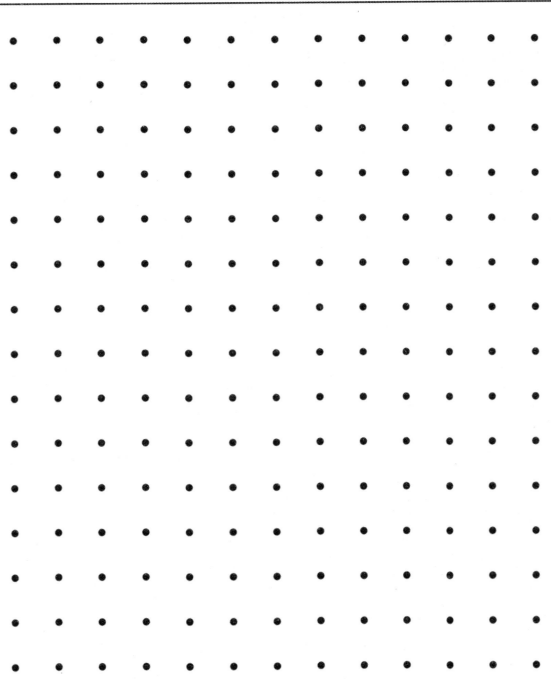

He Would Prepare the Way for
Jesus

Word Search

```
Z E C H A R I A H
Q L W E R T Y U I
O I P A S D F Y A
G Z H J K L B Z N
X A C V B A N M G
B B N M B Q W E E
R E T Y U I O P L
A T E M P L E S D
F H G J O H N H J
```

WORDS TO FIND:

ZECHARIAH   ELIZABETH   TEMPLE

ANGEL   BABY   JOHN

Gabriel Spoke to Joseph in a Dream

A-Mazing!

Can you find you way to the church?

He Took Mary to Be His Wife

Tic-Tac-Toe

One player is X, the other player is O. Take turns marking in one of the nine squares on the board. First to get three in a row wins!

winner _____

winner _____

winner _____

winner _____

Mary and Joseph Go Home to
Bethlehem

Word Search

```
B M J O S E P H E
R E T T Y I O P A
S D T R A V E L F
G H J H K L Z X C
V B N M L Q W E R
T D O N K E Y Y U
I O P A S D H F G
H J K L Z X C E V
H O M E M Y R A M
```

WORDS TO FIND:

BETHLEHEM   JOSEPH   MARY

TRAVEL   DONKEY   HOME

Mary Will Be the Mother of
Jesus

Fill In the Blank:

Read about the birth of Jesus in Luke 1 and 2 and fill in the correct answers in the blanks below

1. God sent the angel _____ to a virgin pledged to be   married to a man named Joseph.

2. The virgin's name was _____.

3. But the angel said to her, "You will give birth to a son, and you are to call him _____.

4. In those days Caesar Augustus issued a decree that a _____   should be taken.

5. _____ also went to Bethlehem... He went there to register   with Mary, who was pledged to be married to him and was expecting a child.

6. While they were there, the time came for the _____ to be born, and she gave birth to her firstborn, a son.

7. She wrapped him in cloths and placed him in a _____, because there was no guest room available for them.

There Was No Room in the Inn

Jesus is Born

The Greatest Word Unscramble!

Try to unscramble the letters on the left to
form the names of the first six books of the New Testament.

THEMAWT   _____

KARM   _____

KULE   _____

NOJH   _____

ASCT   _____

NAMROS   _____

Jesus was Laid in a
Manger

Jesus was wrapped in swaddling clothes. List the different kinds of clothes you wore as a baby!

_____

_____   _____

_____   _____

_____   _____

_____   _____

_____   _____

_____   _____

_____   _____

_____   _____

The Shepherds Watched at **Night**

Fill In the Blank:

Read about the birth of Jesus in Luke 1 and 2 and fill in the correct answers in the blanks below

1. And there were _____ keeping watch over their
flocks at night.

2. An _____ of the Lord appeared to them, and
they were terrified.

3. But the angel said to them, "Do not be afraid. I
bring you _____ _____ that will cause great joy for
all the people.

4. Today a _____ has been born to you; he is the
Messiah, the Lord.

5. Suddenly the heavenly host appeared praising God
and saying, "Glory to ____ in the highest heaven!"

6. The shepherds said to one another, "Let's go to
_____ and see this thing that has happened,
which the Lord has told us about."

7. When they had seen him, they _____ ____
_____ concerning what had been told
them.

1. shepherds 2. Angel 3. good news 4. Savior 5. God 6. Bethlehem 7. spread the word

The Angels Sang
Glory to God

Tic-Tac-Toe

One player is X, the other player is O. Take turns marking in one of the nine squares on the board. First to get three in a row wins!

winner _____

winner _____

winner _____

winner _____

Peace
and Goodwill to Men

count the Angels

How many angels were at Jesus' birth?

Jesus Was Wrapped in Swaddling Clothes

What Do I Say?

Cow says _____

Sheep says _____

Bird says _____

Baby says _____

The Shepherds

Told Everyone About Jesus

A-Mazing!

Help the Wisemen find baby Jesus in the manger!

Help the wise men follow the star!

The wise men need to get to the star before Jesus is born.
Help them find their way!

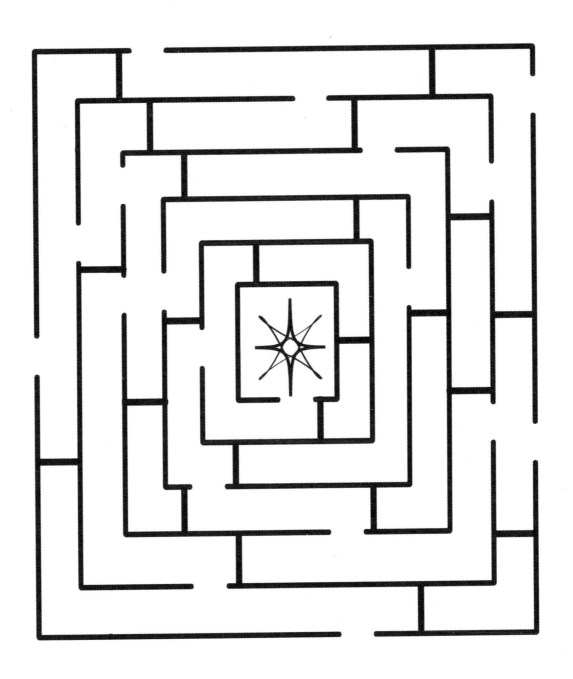

Baby John Grew Up to Be

John the Baptist

fill In the Blank:

Read about John the Baptist in Matthew 3

1. John's clothes were made of _____ _____.

2. He had a leather _____around his waist.

3. His food was locusts and wild _____.

4. John the Baptist came, preaching in the wilderness and saying, "_____!"

5. People were baptized by him in the _____ River.

6. Jesus said, "I tell you the truth, of all who have ever lived, none is greater than _____ ____ _____."

Jesus Brought Salvation to the World

Word Search

Find the list of words at the bottom of the page in this jumble of letters!

```
R  O  J  B  F  E  S  X
P  H  E  A  L  L  I  J
N  K  U  H  R  C  S  D
D  B  L  I  N  D  K  P
E  L  I  M  Y  V  I  O
A  X  E  N  L  O  B  W
F  J  E  S  U  S  N  E
J  U  L  Y  V  D  C  R
```

WORDS TO FIND:

JESUS   POWER   HEAL

BLIND   DEAF

A-Mazing!

Help the shepherds find their sheep!

Christmas Is

Jesus' Birthday

The Great Dot Game!

Each player must draw a line (up and down or side to side, no diagonals) to connect 2 dots on the board. If a player's line closes a square, then they recieve 1 point. If you close a box, you get to draw another line! Write your initials inside any closed boxes to keep track of how many points you have!

Thank You Lord for
Sending Jesus

Tic-Tac-Toe

One player is X, the other player is O. Take turns marking in one of the
nine squares on the board. First to get three in a row wins!

winner _____

winner _____

winner _____

winner _____

Word Search

Find the list of words at the bottom of the page in this jumble of letters!

```
Z E C H A R I A H
B L I C X J O B D
K I H W U V E Y A
C Z D E Y E B A N
O A L P I A M E G
I B J Q B K I J E
M E N L C T S E L
Z T E M P L E S N
A H T J O H N A B
```

WORDS TO FIND:

ZECHARIAH TEMPLE BABY

ANGEL ELIZABETH JOHN

The Reason for the Season!

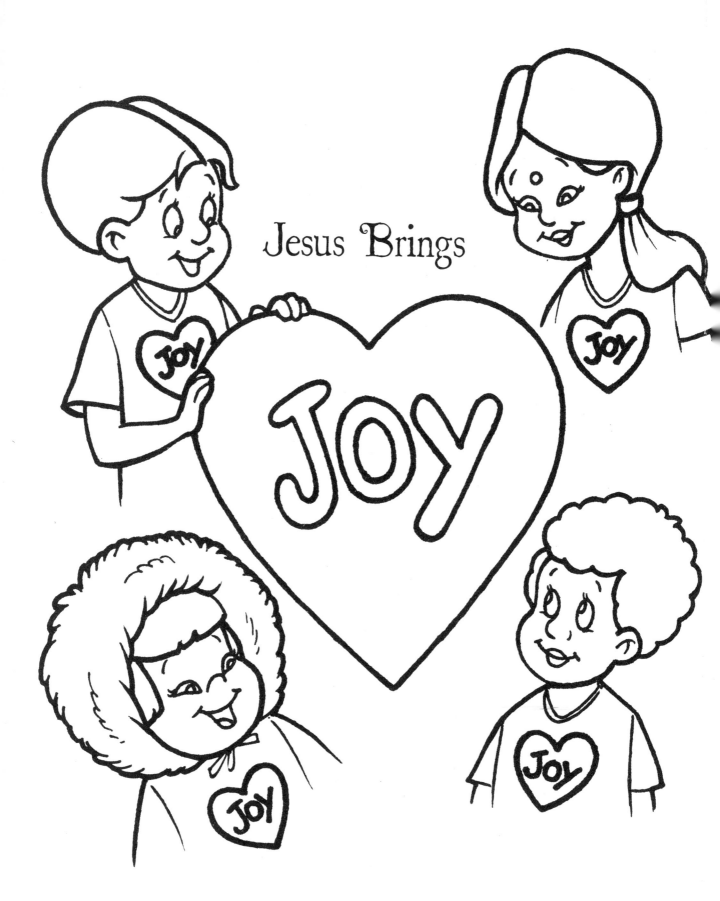

What Gives You Joy?

Draw anything that gives you joy inside the heart!

We Celebrate Jesus By
Singing Carols

Word Search

Find the list of words at the bottom of the page in this jumble of letters!

```
J  I  N  G  L  E  I  A  H
B  J  I  C  X  J  O  B  D
K  O  H  W  U  V  E  L  S
C  Y  D  E  Y  E  R  A  I
O  A  L  P  I  O  M  E  L
I  B  J  Q  W  K  I  J  E
M  E  N  L  C  T  S  E  N
Z  B  E  L  L  S  M  S  T
A  H  T  N  I  G  H  T  B
```

WORDS TO FIND:

JINGLE	BELLS	SILENT
NIGHT	JOY	WORLD

We Celebrate Christmas By
Thanking God

LIST THE THINGS YOU ARE THANKFUL FOR!

_____ | _____ | _____

_____ | _____ | _____

_____ | _____ | _____

_____ | _____ | _____

_____ | _____ | _____

_____ | _____ | _____

Everybody Ought to Know
Jesus

Using only the letters in the words below, how many other words can you make?

JESUS LOVES THE LITTLE CHILDREN

_____   _____

_____   _____

_____   _____

_____   _____

_____   _____

_____   _____

_____   _____

_____   _____

_____   _____

_____   _____

The **Angels**
Sang **Praise**

Fill in the blanks to learn how to praise Him:

1. W__ R __ __ __ __

2. __ __ O __ E

3. __ __ L L __ __ U __ __ __

4. __ __ __G

5. __ __ __Y

6. P__ __ __ __E

Thank God
For His Creations

The Great Dot Game!

Each player must draw a line (up and down or side to side, no diagonals) to connect 2 dots on the board. If a player's line closes a square, then they recieve 1 point. If you close a box, you get to draw another line! Write your initials inside any closed boxes to keep track of how many points you have!

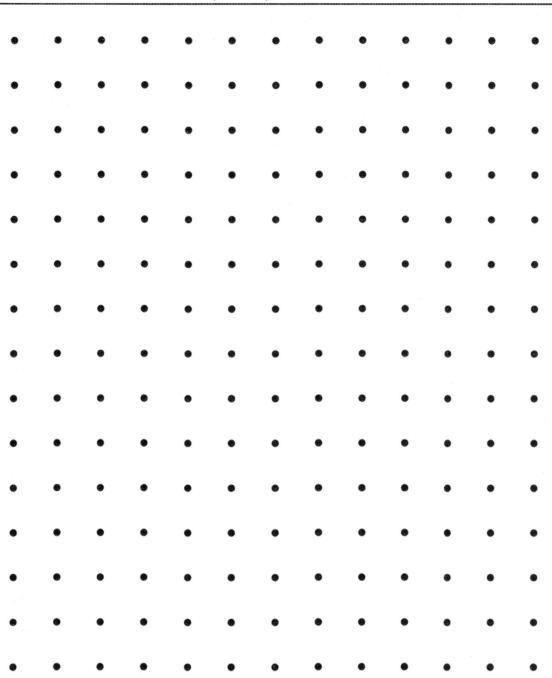

Tell Others About God's Love

Sing Praise

Unscramble the words below to find the titles to some of our favorite Christmas carols:

1. YAWA NI A AMNREG

_____ ____ ___ _____

2. OYJ OT HTE ORDLW

_____ ____ ___ _____ _____

3. SLNITE TIGNH

_____ _____

4. EW HTERE GNKIS

_____ _____ _____

5. HTE IRFTS OENL

_____ _____ _____

6. O ITLTEL WNOT FO THEBELMEH

___ _____ _____ ____

_____

Do What
Jesus Would Do

using only the letters in the words below, how many other words can you make?

JESUS LOVES US ALL

_____ _____

_____ _____

_____ _____

_____ _____

_____ _____

_____ _____

_____ _____

_____ _____

_____ _____

_____ _____

Christmas Means Hearts Full of Joy!

Tic-Tac-Toe

One player is X, the other player is O. Take turns marking in one of the nine squares on the board. First to get three in a row wins!

winner _____

winner _____

winner _____

winner _____

Heaven
Is Real

Word Search

Find the list of words at the bottom of the page in this jumble of letters!

```
H E A V E N I A H
B G I C X J O B D
K A H W U V E L J
H T D E Y E R A E
O E L P I O M E S
M B J Q W K I J U
E E N L C T S E S
Z A N G E L M S T
A H T P R A I S E
```

WORDS TO FIND:

HEAVEN	ANGEL	JESUS
PRAISE	GATE	HOME